Love Letters from God
Walking in the Word

Book Seven

Walking with Jesus

Becoming the Best Me I Can Be

Pamela D White

All scripture quotations, unless otherwise indicated, are taken from the Holy Bible, **New King James Version©**. Copyright © 1982 by Thomas Nelson, Inc. Used by permission. All rights reserved.

Scripture quotations marked NIV are taken from the Holy Bible, **New International Version** ®, NIV ®. Copyright © 1973, 1978, 1984 by **Biblica, Inc.® Used by permission. All rights reserved worldwide.**

Scripture quotations marked NASB are taken from the Holy Bible, **New American Standard Bible®,** Copyright © 1960, 1971, 1977, 1995, 2020 by The Lockman Foundation. All rights reserved.

Scripture quotations marked AMP are taken from the Holy Bible, **Amplified**, copyright © 2015 by The Lockman Foundation, La Habra, CA 90631. All rights reserved. For Permission To Quote information visit http://www.lockman.org/

Scripture quotations marked ESV are taken from the ESV® Bible (The Holy Bible, **English Standard Version**®). ESV® Text Edition: 2016. Copyright © 2001 by Crossway, a publishing ministry of Good News Publishers. The ESV® text has been reproduced in cooperation with and by permission of Good News Publishers. Unauthorized reproduction of this publication is prohibited. All rights reserved.

Scripture quotations marked NLT are taken from the Holy Bible, **New Living Translation**, copyright © 1996, 2004, 2015 by Tyndale House Foundation. Used by permission of Tyndale House Publishers, Inc., Carol Stream, Illinois 60188. All rights reserved.

Scripture quotations marked MSG are taken from **THE MESSAGE**, copyright © 1993, 2002, 2018 by Eugene H. Peterson. Used by permission of NavPress. All rights reserved. Represented by Tyndale House Publishers, Inc.

Scripture quotations marked AKJV are taken from the Holy Bible, **Authorized King James Version**, The Authorized (King James) Version of the Bible ('the KJV'), the rights in which are vested in the Crown in the United Kingdom, is reproduced here by permission of the Crown's patentee, Cambridge University Press. The Cambridge KJV text, including paragraphing, is reproduced here by permission of Cambridge University Press.

Scripture quotations marked KJV are taken from the Holy Bible, **King James Version**.

A publication of Blooming Desert Ministries

ISBN 978-1-7370803-2-9 (sc print)
ISBN 978-1-7370803-3-6 (ebook)

Printed in the United States of America
Copyright © 2021 by Pamela D White
All Rights Reserved.

IngramSparks Publishing (Ingram: Lightning Source, LLC)

One Ingram Blvd., La Vergne, TN 37086

Publishing Note: Publishing style capitalizes certain pronouns in Scriptures that refer to the Father, Son, and Holy Spirit, and may differ from other publishing styles. **All emphasis in the Scriptures' quotations is the authors.** The name satan and related names are not capitalized as the author's preference not to acknowledge him, even though it violates grammatical rules.

No part of this book may be reproduced or transmitted in any form or by any means, electronic or mechanical – including photocopying, recording, or by any information storage and retrieval system – without permission in writing from the publisher. Please direct inquires to PDW Publications.

PDW PUBLICATIONS

Dedication

This book series is dedicated to you.

Everyone has opportunities to become a better version of themselves. My prayer is that this book series helps you on that journey. The Lord loves you so much He desires an intimate relationship with you. You are special to Him and He loves spending time with you. Walking and talking with Jesus every day should be the norm, not the exception. Life can bring difficult circumstances and situations. When you walk with Jesus, life events, are not only manageable but can be turned for your good.

"And we know that all things work together for good to those who love God, to those who are the called according to His purpose," Romans 8:28.

Come with me into this exploration of how you can develop a relationship with Jesus and walk with Him every day. This is an opportunity to become a better you.

Acknowledgments

The Great Commission given by our Lord and Savior Jesus Christ noted in Matthew 28:16-20 is my inspiration for this publication. Verses 19-20 state, *"Go therefore and make disciples of all the nations, baptizing them in the name of the Father and of the Son and of the Holy Spirit, teaching them to observe all things that I have commanded you; and lo, I am with you always, even to the end of the age."* This verse is the very basis for missionary work all over the globe. I have been blessed to be able to serve in a few of those missions. Missions are an amazing experience. I came to realize though that everyone cannot always do all the parts commanded in these verses. I can't always go. I didn't often get to baptize. What I realized was that I can do my part in teaching to observes the truths of the Scriptures. My desire to fulfill the teaching part of the Great Commission was the inspiration for this work. My pastor, Bishop Larry Taylor, and First Lady Desetra Taylor allowed our church to use these Bible studies in our New Life Discipleship classes for nearly twenty years. The work has also been used in prison ministries in central Illinois for as many years. The teaching has proven effective in changing many lives and discipling the children of God. Thank you, Bishop and First Lady, for teaching a balanced spiritual and natural life so I could complete this project and see the impact of the work on people's lives.

Bishop positioned me to be the director of New Life Ministries Discipleship for several years. New Life classes were designed to teach those new to Christianity or new to the church the foundational truths needed to build a solid life in Christ. During that time, this work was fine-tuned with the help and input from the dedicated, gifted, and anointed New Life teachers Minister Retta Smith, Minister James Smith, Minister Debby Henkel, Dr. Terry Husband, Minister Char-Michelle McDowell, Minister Yvonne Smith, Minister Herbert Smyer, and Professor Susan Gibson along with the encouragement and guidance of Dr. Chequita Brown and community service advocate Minister Patricia Turner. I also want to give a shout-out to Dr. Wanda Turner, nationally acclaimed minister, teacher, prophet, life coach, mentor, and best-selling author, who continued to encourage me to just publish the thing! Thanks to all of you. Each of you has made a significant impact on my life.

My dear friend and mentor, First Lady Marshell Wickware, supported the project and pushed me to publish it for years. Thanks for not giving up on me!

My life-long friend, Robin McClallen, thank you for all your support, input, and encouraging me to publish something. You have been instrumental in making me an author.

A special thanks to my husband, Brian K. White, for his patience and prayers as I spent hours and hours researching, writing, and rewriting. Thanks, BW!

Most of all thank you to the Holy Spirit and my Lord and Savior Jesus Christ. I present this work in obedience and honor to You.

Contents

Introduction	11
Why the Bible is Important	13
Basic Bible Structure	17
Old Testament	18
Pentateuch	18
Historical	18
Poetry	20
Prophets	20
Major Prophets	21
Minor Prophets	21
New Testament	23
Gospels	23
Historical	23
Epistles	24
Prophetic	26
Religious or Spiritual	29
How to Approach the Bible	33
Practical Help	35
Heart Conditions	39
Understanding Context	43
Memorization	45
Summing It Up	49
Helpful Tools	51

Stepping Stones	53
Love Letters from God	55
Glossary	57
About the Author	63

Chapter Seven

Love Letters from God
Walking in the Word

OBJECTIVE

This chapter presents the importance of daily Bible meditation and provides tools for developing your relationship with the Lord through His Word.

MEMORY VERSE

"This Book of the Law shall not depart from your mouth, but you shall meditate in it day and night, that you may observe to do according to all that is written in it. For then you will make your way prosperous, and then you will have good success," Joshua 1:8.

Love Letters from God

A. **Why the Bible is Important**

B. **Basic Bible Structure**
   1. Old Testament
      a. Pentateuch
      b. Historical
      c. Poetry
      d. Prophets—Major and Minor
   2. New Testament
      a. Gospels
      b. Historical
      c. Epistles
      d. Prophetic

C. **Religious or Spiritual**

D. **How to Approach the Bible**

E. **Practical Help**

F. **Heart Conditions**

G. **Understanding Context**

H. **Memorization**

I. **Summing It Up**

J. **Helpful Tools**

Chapter Seven
Love Letters from God
Walking in the Word
Introduction

One tool we have discussed in every chapter that can powerfully assist you in life is the Word of God or the Bible. Reading the Bible can seem like a very daunting task. The Bible is not an ordinary book; it is the inspired Word of God. The Word lives and breathes and has the power to change your life. Reading the Bible differs from reading any other book. The Bible is a love letter from your Father and Creator. In His love letter to you, He has included everything you need to know about life and godliness. It might not seem like accounts of ancient battles and strange-sounding prophecies from bearded old men could help you through the struggles you have today. Ecclesiastes 1:9 says, *"That which has been is what will be, that which is done is what will be done, and there is nothing new under the sun."* You may not be conducting war against a Philistine army, but the lessons learned in the various experiences in the Bible apply to overcoming life's struggles, maturing in Christ, and living a life of security and peace, even if everything around you is chaos. Every book of the Bible offers insight into how to deal with everyday life. God wants you to have the tools to make wise choices in your life. The Word holds the answers to how God desires to develop a relationship with you, His special creation, and His plan for your future.

Why the Bible is Important

It is important to understand and believe that the Bible does not have any errors and is a God-inspired message to you specifically. Doubting the Word robs you of the insight and wisdom available to you through the Bible. God used forty human authors whom He inspired to record the message God wants to be heard. So if people wrote the Bible, then why aren't there any errors? There are no errors because God divinely inspired the writing of the Bible. God may have used imperfect people to pen the Words, but the message is perfect because it is from Him. The message of the Bible tells the story of Jesus from Genesis to Revelation, exposes and corrects decisions and behaviors, shows you the right way to live and how to make choices that support righteousness and holiness. The Bible brings glory to God and increases your faith. Most of all, the Bible develops your relationship with the Lord. Intertwined in every story is the love of God. I know it might seem weird to say that stories of wars, struggle, lopping off heads, and rampant disease are part of a love letter. But I promise, if you open your heart, you will find why the Lord sent that message to you and you will know the love that the message delivered.

"All Scripture is given by inspiration of God, and is profitable for doctrine, for reproof, for correction, for instruction in righteousness," 2 Timothy 3:16.

Many scriptures support the importance of being intimate with the message in the Bible and the power of the Word of God. Here are a few:

- *"Be diligent to present yourself approved to God, a worker who does not need to be ashamed, rightly dividing the Word of truth,"* 2 Timothy 2:15.

- *"Forever, O Lord, thy Word is settled in heaven,"* Psalms 119:89.

- *"I will worship toward Your holy temple, and praise Your name for Your lovingkindness and Your truth; for You have magnified Your Word above all Your name,"* Psalms 138:2.

- *"For whatever things were written before were written for our learning, that we through the patience and comfort of the Scriptures might have hope,"* Romans 15:4.

- *"The grass withers, the flower fades, but the Word of our God stands forever"* Isaiah 40:8.

- *"For assuredly, I say to you, till heaven and earth pass away, one jot or one tittle will by no means pass from the law till all is fulfilled,"* Matthew 5:18.

- *"Heaven and earth will pass away, but My Words will by no means pass away,"* Matthew 24:35.

- *"But the Word of the Lord endures forever." Now this is the Word which by the gospel was preached to you,"* I Peter 1:25.

- *"Man lives by the Word of God,"* Deuteronomy 8:3.

- *"So He humbled you, allowed you to hunger, and fed you with manna which you did not know nor did your fathers know, that He might *make you know that man shall not live by bread alone; but man lives by every Word that proceeds from the mouth of the Lord,"* Job 23:12.

- *"How sweet are Your Words to my taste, sweeter than honey to my mouth!"* Psalm 119:103.

- *"Your Words were found, and I ate them, and Your Word was to me the joy and rejoicing of my heart; for I am called by Your name, O Lord God of hosts,"* Jeremiah 15:16.

- *"As newborn babes, desire the pure milk of the Word, that you may grow thereby,"* 1 Peter 2:2.

- *"All Scripture is given by inspiration of God, and is profitable for doctrine, for reproof, for correction, for instruction in righteousness,"* 2 Timothy 3:16.

- *"In the beginning was the Word, and the Word was with God, and the Word was God,"* John 1:1.

- *"I will meditate on Your precepts, and contemplate Your ways,"* Psalm 119:15.

- *"And I will walk at liberty, for I seek Your precepts,"* Psalm 119: 45.

Basic Bible Structure

We are going to look at the structure of the Bible only so you know how it's put together. Sometimes it's important to know who wrote a book of the Bible and when it was written, so you can understand references in the historical accounts. The Bible is a manuscript composed of multiple smaller books. We divide the Bible into two sections, the Old Testament and the New Testament. Testament means covenant. A covenant is a promise between two parties. These two sections explain the first covenants and the newer covenant of Christ. Each Testament is divided into subdivisions called books. There are sixty-six (66) total books in the Bible. The testaments are divided into thirty-nine (39) books in the Old Testament and twenty-seven (27) books in the New Testament. Each book is divided into chapters and each chapter is divided into verses. The verses are numbered for easy reference. Sometimes when you read, a hard stop happens at chapters or verses as if that was the intended break. However, remember that was not how it was written. Many of the books in the New Testament were letters written to people or churches. When you write a letter, do you break it into chapters and verses? Of course not, and neither did the authors of the letters in the New Testament. The breaks are simply for ease of reference. When you read, allow the Lord to guide you because He may not want you to stop at the end of a chapter so you can get the full message of what He is conveying to you that day. The Old Testament books are not letters like the New Testament but are historical accounts of things that occurred. Again, the chapters and verses were added for ease of reference and were not part of the original writing.

Old Testament

The Old Testament was originally written in the Hebrew language, with some written in Aramaic. Bible writing spans the years between about 1200 -100 BC. The message of the Bible, however, is timeless.

Pentateuch

The Old Testament begins with five books written by the patriarch, Moses. They are called the **Pentateuch** or the Five Books of the Law. The Jewish faith calls these five books the Torah.

- Genesis: How God's relationship with man began.
- Exodus: God delivers Israel from slavery in Egypt.
- Leviticus: God's instructions on how to worship Him.
- Numbers: Israelites wander in the desert when their faith fails.
- Deuteronomy: God instructs on how to love and obey Him in the Promised Land.

Historical

The next twelve books in the Old Testament are **HISTORICAL** books written by various authors over approximately 1,000 years.

- Joshua: The Israelites enter the Promised Land and receive their inheritance.
- Judges: Israelites repeatedly cycle through serving God, turning away from God, falling captive to enemy nations, calling out to God, being delivered by God through His judges, then serving God again.
- Ruth: The story of two widows, hope, and redemption.
- 1 Samuel: Israel decides they want to be ruled by kings.
- 2 Samuel: David becomes king and builds the kingdom of Israel.
- 1 Kings: The kingdom of Israel splits into two kingdoms - Judah and Israel.
- 2 Kings: Both kingdoms ignore God and end up in captivity to major world empires.
- 1 Chronicles: A recap of history from Adam to King David.
- 2 Chronicles: A continuation of history from David to Babylonian captivity.
- Ezra: Israelites return to Jerusalem and rebuild the temple once again serving the Lord.
- Nehemiah: Nehemiah returns to Jerusalem to rebuild the wall around the city, showing you what it is like to have the Holy Spirit rebuild your life when you accept Jesus in your life.
- Esther: The account of a queen who saves the Israelites from genocide and an example of divine destiny.

Poetry

These first seventeen books, the Law and History books, deal with the morality and development of the nation of Israel. The people are learning how to function in relationships with one another and with Jehovah God, the great I AM. The next five books deal with the human heart and experience. They are the heartbeat of the scriptures as they show how to apply spiritual insight to everyday situations. They are called books of **POETRY**.

- Job: The story of a man named Job who is a faithful servant of the Lord who endures much suffering at the hand of Satan.

- Psalms: Songs of praise and worship to God.

- Proverbs: A collection of wise saying to help you through life.

- Ecclesiastes: Shows you how depressing and devastating a life without God can be.

- Song of Solomon: A celebration of love.

Prophets

The last books of the Old Testament are prophetic. These books are divided into two sections, the Major and the Minor **PROPHETS**. This doesn't mean that the Major Prophets are more important than the Minor Prophets. Calling these books major or minor refers to the length of the books, not their importance. The Hebrews, because of the order of the books in the Bible, classified these prophetic books as Latter Prophets. There are prophets throughout the Bible from Genesis to Revelation and are mixed in with historical accounts. These books focus on specific prophets and their prophetic insight or foresight of things that pertain to the future. The prophets functioned as watchmen over Israel, preachers of the Mosaic law, and predictors of events about the Messiah and the Kingdom of God. Sometimes they were called seers because they saw things that were to come.

Major Prophets

- Isaiah: Isaiah warns about sin, judgment to come, and a soon and coming king that would save the world, a.k.a. Jesus Christ.

- Jeremiah: Jeremiah warns Israel about the coming Babylonian captivity.

- Lamentations: Israel left God and suffered captivity because of it. Now they are complaining to God because of their suffering.

- Ezekiel: God sends Ezekiel to His people to teach them what they did wrong so they could live in righteous justice.

- Daniel: Daniel has many visions of the future of Israel.

Minor Prophets

- Hosea: God tells Hosea to marry a prostitute who keeps leaving him to go back to her insidious lifestyle to give you a picture of what His relationship with Israel is like.

- Joel: Joel tells you that salvation is coming to the sinner along with God's favor.

- Amos: A shepherd preacher tells about the injustices that are occurring and the purity God expects.

- Obadiah: A prophetic vision telling the arrogant descendants of Esau about the charges against them for the violence they showed Israel.

- Jonah: The prophet Jonah shows the compassion of God to a pagan nation, after a few days in a big fish.

- Micah: Micah prophesies the coming Messiah and His rule in perfect peace.

- Nahum: Nahum shows that God is slow to anger, unrepented sin will be punished, and God protects those who love Him.

- Habakkuk: Habakkuk shows that God expects absolute trust.

- Zephaniah: The Day of the Lord is coming, and God's desire is for you to live in peace and justice.

- Haggai: As people return to restoring the temple, God shows He is in the business of restoration of His children.

- Zechariah: Zechariah prophecies our God, Yahweh, is returning grace, forgiveness, and love.

- Malachi: Malachi reminds us that God is always faithful and calls His people to honor the covenant of God.

This brings us to the end of the Old Testament. Between the end of the Old Testament and the beginning of the New Testament are about 400 years. The Israelites have been living under the Mosaic Law for hundreds of years. They are primed and ready for the appearance of the Messiah.

New Testament

The twenty-seven books of the New Testament begin with four books called the Gospels. The men who wrote the **Gospels** were eyewitnesses of Jesus' ministry and had a personal relationship with Him.

Gospels

Gospel means the teaching or revelation of Christ. The four Gospels are all about things that happened while Jesus walked the earth.

- Matthew: Matthew's account of Jesus' life, death, burial, and resurrection showing Jesus as Son of God and King of Israel.

- Mark: Mark portrays Jesus as the Messiah, a servant with authority who ransomed His life for humankind.

- Luke: As Luke carefully chronicles the life of Jesus, he shows you that Jesus is the fulfillment of the Old Testament prophecies of the Messianic Deliverer that was to come.

- John: John's book tells of Jesus, who is the divine incarnation of God and comes as goodness and love.

Historical

After these four Gospel accounts of Jesus, find the New Testament **Historical** book. The book of Acts records the birth of the church, the coming of the Holy Spirit, and the fulfillment of the command of Jesus for the Apostles to go into other nations and preach the Gospel.

- Acts: The book of acts is a letter that Luke wrote to Theophilus about Jesus returning to the Father, the promised Holy Spirit coming, and the spread of the Gospel of Christ. It is a historical account of the beginning of Christianity.

Epistles

The next twenty-one books of the New Testament are called Epistles. The Word epistle means letter or message. They are letters written to churches and individuals. Thirteen of the letters are known as the Pauline Epistles. Paul wrote Ephesians, Philippians, Colossians, and Philemon while imprisoned for preaching about Jesus. Some of Paul's letters are written to specific churches. Three of Paul's letters are Pastoral Epistles written to pastors of churches. Paul wrote a fourth letter from prison to his friend, Philemon. The rest of the letters in the New Testament are General Epistles, written to a universal audience.

- Romans: Paul theologically presents an explanation of the Gospel to the Roman churches to refute some skewed religious thinking.

- 1 Corinthians: The churches in the Greek city of Corinth were practicing some unacceptable behaviors, which Paul corrects in this letter, showing them true discipleship.

- 2 Corinthians: Paul again writes to the Corinthian church admonishing them to repent, forgive, be reconciled to Christ, and live in grace.

- Galatians: Paul writes to the church in Galatia, teaching them the difference between living by the law versus living by faith.

- Ephesians: Paul writes to the church in Ephesus in the Roman Empire teaching them to be light in the darkness living in peace and love through the grace of God obtained by faith.

- Philippians: Paul writes to the church in Philippi, encouraging them to walk in the joy of the Lord.

- Colossians: Paul writes to the church in Colossae, telling them of the supremacy of Jesus Christ in all creation, the works of men, and daily life.

- 1 Thessalonians: Paul writes to the church in Thessalonica encouraging them to be faithful followers of Christ so they are ready for the Day of the Lord, the return of Christ.

- 2 Thessalonians: The Thessalonians have been fighting hard, defending their faith. Paul encourages them to not grow weary but stand strong in their faith.

- 1 Timothy: Timothy is Paul's protégé. In this letter Paul wrote to Timothy, Paul gives Timothy instructions on how to pastor the church Timothy is leading.

- 2 Timothy: Again, Paul writes to Timothy, this time to encourage Timothy and charge him to keep up the faith even after Paul is gone.

- Titus: Paul writes to Titus, instructing him how to maintain order and have an effective ministry to the church on the island of Crete.

- Philemon: Paul writes to Philemon about how to deal with Philemon's runaway slave.

- Hebrews: As the Gospel spread, persecution increased. The letter to the Hebrews lets them know there is a High Priest, Jesus Christ, who sees what is happening and feels their struggle. Paul encourages the Hebrews to trust and have faith in Jesus.

- James: James encourages believers to not just believe but to put feet to their faith and be doers of the Word putting action to their faith.

- 1 Peter: Peter writes to the church, encouraging them to live holy by the Spirit of God despite persecution.

- 2 Peter: Peter reminds the church, Jesus is returning, the Day of the Lord is coming and they need to prepare themselves for that day believing the promises of God and being aware of false teachers who would attempt to deceive them.

- 1 John: The Apostle John writes to the Christians about the importance of developing a relationship with the Lord.

- 2 John: Another letter from John encouraging Christians to walk in love, truth, and obedience.

- 3 John: A brief letter from John to Gaius encouraging walking in truth and supporting other Christians.

- Jude: Another half-brother of Jesus, Jude, encourages Christians to contend for the faith despite persecutions and false teachers while striving for godliness and the promises of God.

PROPHETIC

The last book of the New Testament is the book of Revelation. Revelation is a **PROPHETIC** book written by the Apostle John while he was exiled on the Greek island of Patmos. It is a book full of colorful descriptions of things that have not yet occurred as the world we know comes to an end.

- Revelation: John writes the vision of things yet to come, bringing the Bible to a close. Jesus is the Alpha and Omega, beginning and end.

Religious or Spiritual

Now that you know a little about this amazing love letter from God, it's time to take the step to include it in your life. There is no formula or right/wrong way to start. The important thing is that you incorporate the Bible into your life. You know your schedule, the best way you learn and remember, your time constraints, and family situations so only you can find the best way to approach your Bible meditation time.

The time spent in the Word of God will help you get to know your God on an intimate level. Some religions teach Christians should do good works and the more good works you do, the more likely you will be to get into heaven and earn great rewards. Heaven does have glorious rewards for good works, but you don't do good works to get there. You do good works because Christ lives in you. Good works don't save you; Jesus saves you. Paul had to remind the Ephesians of this in his letter to the church *"For by grace you have been saved through faith, and that not of yourselves; it is the gift of God, not of works, lest anyone should boast,"* Ephesians 2:8-9. You want to be careful of falling into this trap and read the Bible because it seems like a good thing to do. The Bible is a gift to be cherished. Jesus is the Word. *"In the beginning was the Word, and the Word was with God, and the Word was God. He was in the beginning with God.*

All things were made through Him, and without Him nothing was made that was made. In Him was life, and the life was the light of men," John 1:1-4. Spending time in the Scriptures is spending time with Jesus. It's like sitting over coffee with your best friend. It's intimate and personal.

In the Gospels, we see Jesus getting angry with the Pharisees. Jewish people revered the Pharisees as religious leaders. Why would He be so angry with the very people who were teaching others the precious Words of Moses and the prophets? He was angry because they had become so deeply religious; they were no longer spiritual. Then they put strict rules and laws on everyone else so they too were caught in the bondage of religion. Let's look at the difference between religion and spirituality. Religion teaches a code of ethics and laws. It is dependent on doing good works. Religion is about tons of self-effort. There is a lot of head knowledge and theology brought by teachers and instructors and other eternal means. Religion reaches you on a conscious level. There is a lot of guilt associated with religion because it's just impossible to live like religion wants you to live.

Spiritual Christianity is all about Father, Son, and Holy Spirit. A Christian led by the Spirit does not need a code of ethics or a long list of laws because the power of the Holy Spirit guides to righteous decisions and intimacy with the Father is a life that lives the law from within instead of one who tries to follow the law from a decision. Where religion is about works, spiritual Christianity is about intimacy with the Lord. *"But seek ye first the kingdom of God, and his righteousness; and all these things shall be added unto you,"* Matthew 6:33 KJV. His heart's desire is that you seek Him, not try to prove yourself through works. As you seek Him, truth becomes illuminated, and you have deep spiritual encounters, which far surpass any theology. You have the power of the Holy Spirit guiding your life. You can throw out self-help books and self-effort. The Holy Spirit will empower you and fill you with strength. Instead of only being conscious of the things surrounding you, a spiritual Christian will be aware of the constant communication and communion with the Lord throughout their day.

Balance is important in everything you do. The same is true for your journey through the Bible. To get too religious about it will make you like the Pharisees, so caught up in keeping the Law that you miss the Messiah. They had the Bible, but no Spirit. Another extreme is to be too spiritual without the anchor of the Bible. This can lead you into New Age thinking and practices that will move you into idolatry with false gods. True Christianity is a perfect balance between Bible and Spirit. The Bible is important, and the Spirit is important. To reject either will lead you astray from the Truth.

How to Approach the Bible

You always want to remain **HUMBLE** in the presence of the Lord. The Lord instructs you to come to Him as little children. *"Truly, I say to you, unless you turn and become like children, you will never enter the kingdom of heaven,"* Matthew 18:3 ESV.

You also want to approach the Bible in **FAITH** that the Word of God is true, that you can learn the ways of God, develop to be more like Christ, grow in the power of the Spirit and God's love.

You want to learn to **ABIDE** in the Word. This is true discipleship, *"So Jesus said to the Jews who had believed him, "If you abide in my Word, you are truly my disciples,"* John 8:31 ESV. To 'abide' means that you decide to continue in the Word, accept its truths, and stand strong in the Word no matter what comes your way.

You want to remember, even when reading a story that might seem violent or troubling, that somewhere in there is a message of God's **LOVE**. If you ask Him, He will show you.

As you become more intimate with the Lord and experience His love for you, then you will show **LOVE TO OTHERS**. *"A new commandment I give* *to you, that you love one another; as I have loved you, that you also love one another. By this all will know that you are My disciples, if you have love for one another,"* John 13:34-35.

You want to always be **SENSITIVE** to the Holy Spirit. As you learned in the Holy Spirit chapter, the Spirit is not pushy. Holy Spirit is gentle. If you are sensitive to His promptings while in the Scriptures, you will receive a flow of revelation.

Some things in the Bible may be difficult to understand. If you don't understand something, you have a superior teacher ready to help you **INTERPRET** the Bible. The Holy Spirit loves to open up the scriptures to show you hidden treasures in the Word of God.

Practical Help

Before we look at some practical tips for scripture meditation, we need to talk about the word meditation. Bible scholars and teachers will tell you to study the Bible: analyze, investigate, examine, dissect, philosophize, theologize, and reason, reason, reason. However, the scriptures do not have any instruction on Bible that kind of Bible study. There are, however, hundreds of verses about meditating on the Word of God. Often in the Western world, when describing meditation, the picture is of sitting with legs crossed muttering something and emptying your mind so some spirit can speak to you. That is not Biblical meditation and is contrary to the Word of God. Biblical meditation is prayerfully reflecting on the Word of God, inviting the Holy Spirit to illumine your understanding with pictures, words, and feelings while opening your heart, your spiritual eyes and ears, and your mind to the truths of God. And you don't have to sit on the floor!

Below are a few tips designed to assist you in integrating the Bible into your daily routine.

- Purposely set aside time each day to spend time in the Bible. Start somewhere. Five minutes, ten minutes, thirty minutes, an hour, or whatever time you can allot. Just make sure you make time every day with the sole purpose of devoting that time to spend time with Him in the Word. My favorite time of day is early in the morning. You find what works for you and make that your time to be with the Lord. I can guarantee that as you get to know Him better and grow in your relationship with Him, your five minutes with him will multiply exponentially and hours with Him will feel like moments.

- Read slowly, take your time. Rushing just to get through a certain amount of verses or chapters will cause you to miss the message God has for you that day. If you follow a Bible reading plan, they often have you read at least three Old Testament chapters and one New Testament chapter and perhaps a Psalm or Proverb every day. I have often used Bible reading plans to help keep me on track. However, if the Lord illuminates a scripture for you, take your time, and don't feel guilty if you get stuck on one verse, one chapter, or one section. God probably has an important lesson there for you today. Just pick up tomorrow where you left off. I promise you that the Lord would rather have you stop and meditate on the scripture He had jump off the page for you that will change your life than have you struggle to read designated chapters and glean nothing.

- Protect your time to meditate alone so you have personal time to communicate with the Lord. He desires to be with you and will meet with you each day, just like He walked with Adam in the Garden of Eden every day. The Lord loves His creation and enjoys spending time with those He loves, which includes YOU.

- It is also beneficial to interact with others. This can give you insight into things you are struggling with as you explore various concepts. Your faith will grow and you will help others grow in their faith. You might attend a weekly Bible study at your church or join a Bible study group or prayer group.

- There are many ways to approach the Bible. Try not to jump around too much by reading isolated chapters or verses, but explore longer passages, entire books, or specific topics. For instance, perhaps you had a negative report from the doctor. Look up all the scriptures you can find on healing. Write the ones that jump out on some note cards. Carry them around with you, pulling them out at every opportunity and letting them minister to you. The Lord is great at directing you to where you need to be reading. Ask Him!

- Prepare a place just for your study time. People who enjoy and are inspired by the Word are usually those who set aside a regular time and place for Bible meditation. A proper atmosphere will assist you in reaping the complete benefits of your time with the Lord. Find a place that is comfortable and where you like to be. Choose a quiet place free of distractions and concentrate on one thing at a time. I often use instrumental music playing softly in the background to keep a peaceful atmosphere.

- Have all your tools available. You will need your Bible, a notebook or journal, a Bible dictionary, and a concordance. Electronic or physical, you will want these items ready so you won't have to look for them when you need them. When the Lord has a scripture pop out at me, not only do I ask Him about it but I look up meanings of words so I don't interpret it with my Western ideas, but understand the passage's true meaning.

Heart Conditions

There are a couple of things we need to look at regarding heart conditions. Let's take a look at the preparation of the heart. God is always looking at the condition of your heart. When you approach the Bible with a heart ready to connect to Him and hear what He has to communicate to you, the peace and revelation you receive will be astounding.

- Do you have anything to confess? If you do, now is the time to talk to Him about it. **Lord, cleanse me with the power of Your blood**. It's difficult to receive from God if unconfessed things are burdening your heart. You don't need to be embarrassed or ashamed. He has already seen it and knows you did it so you aren't surprising Him. However, He wants you to ask for forgiveness. It's like taking a shower before a big date. Get yourself all cleaned up before you go meet the Lord. Receiving divine revelation is the very heart of biblical meditation, but you can't receive the revelation when sin is blocking the way. Confession opens the way for revelation.

    "Behold, the Lord's hand is not shortened, that it cannot save; nor His ear heavy, that it cannot hear. But your iniquities have separated you

from your God; and your sins have hidden His face from you, so that He will not hear," Isaiah 59:1-2.

- Approach reading the Bible prayerfully. Pray for understanding while being sensitive to the Holy Spirit. Understanding is not always immediate. Sometimes understanding comes with patience. Ask the Holy Spirit to help bring understanding. **LORD, PLEASE GIVE ME A TEACHABLE ATTITUDE**. The Holy Spirit that dwells within you will teach you and empower you to receive the message that is being communicated in your Bible meditation time. Allow the Holy Spirit to reveal truths. Those truths will bring deliverance, guidance, encouragement, healing and so much more.

"But He gives more grace. Therefore He says: 'God resists the proud, but gives grace to the humble,'" James 4:6.

- Slow down and marinate in the Word. Soak it in and allow it to work in you. God gave you a mind, intelligence. The world tells you that your mind is for you to reason and analyze. The Word tells you that your mind should be subject to the Lord in humility so He can renew it and fill it with a revelation of Truth. Ask Him, **"LORD, SHOW ME."**

"I beseech you therefore, brethren, by the mercies of God, that you present your bodies a living sacrifice, holy, acceptable to God, which is your reasonable service. And do not be conformed to this world, but be transformed by the renewing of your mind, that you may prove what is that good and acceptable and perfect will of God," Romans 12:1-2.

- Allow the creativity of God to help you understand. He may anoint your reason, bring a song to mind, flow in pictures or speak to you. God can use anything to illuminate Scripture. **LORD, PLEASE OPEN THE EYES OF MY HEART THAT I MIGHT LEARN OF YOU.**

"Open my eyes, that I may see wondrous things from Your law," Psalm 119:18.

"That the God of our Lord Jesus Christ, the Father of glory, may give to you the spirit of wisdom and revelation in the knowledge of Him, the eyes of your understanding being enlightened; that you may know what is the hope of His calling, what are the riches of the glory of His inheritance in the saints," Ephesians 1:17-18.

- You know how to reason and analyze. Meditating on the word is asking God to flood your reasoning with the river of God. Music may help you. God will give you dreams and visions. Speaking the Word helps keep you balanced and writing what the Lord has illumined and what the Lord reveals will help you remember and give you reference to go back to remind yourself. **LORD, I GIVE TO YOU MY IMAGINATION AND ABILITY TO REASON. HOLY SPIRIT, PLEASE FILL ME AND FLOW THROUGH ME.**

"On the last day, that great day of the feast, Jesus stood and cried out, saying, "If anyone thirsts, let him come to Me and drink. He who believes in Me, as the Scripture has said, out of his heart will flow rivers of living water." But this He spoke concerning the Spirit, whom those believing in Him would receive; for the Holy Spirit was not yet given, because Jesus was not yet glorified," John 7:37-39.

- Some days God may lead you where He wants you to go. It is helpful, though, to have a plan prepared. Your plan should have a purpose and be without presuppositions. Many people like to use devotionals or Bible reading plans as a daily guideline. You may like to pick a specific subject such as healing or finances and allow God to enlarge your understanding and revelation. Maybe you have a specific issue or problem that you need an answer to and focus on receiving an answer to that problem. All those approaches work great! **LORD, SHOW ME THE WAY. WHAT IS THE SOLUTION?** Just remember to keep your heart open to the leading and guidance of the Holy Spirit and read with a focused purpose. Be hungry and thirsty for Him in your life.

"Blessed are those who hunger and thirst for righteousness, for they shall be filled," Matthew 5:6.

"O God, You are my God; early will I seek You; my soul thirsts for You; my flesh longs for You in a dry and thirsty land where there is no water," Psalm 63:1.

- Remember to glorify God for all the insights He gave you. Thank Him! **THANK YOU, LORD, FOR WHAT YOU REVEALED TO ME!**

"You are my God, and I will praise You; You are my God, I will exalt You," Psalm 118:28.

"I give thanks to you, O Lord my God, with my whole heart, and I will glorify your name forever," Psalm 86:12.

Understanding Context

Understanding the context of Scripture may help in understanding the truth of the Word. Here are some questions to consider to stay within the context of a scripture, a passage, or a book. I like to write the answers to these questions in the margin of my Bible. Use a journal, notebook or keep an online record of the following information as you study each book or passage. You may have a Bible that already answers these questions at the beginning of each book of the Bible. We have already talked about not getting analytical or stuck in reasoning. That was what kept the Pharisees stuck. Sometimes, it does help to know who wrote something and why they initially wrote it. Then you can ask the Lord how it pertains to you today. Here are a few questions to ask about each book or passage.

- Who wrote it?
- Who was it written to?
- What are the main events?
- When was it written?
- Where was this done/said/happen?
- Why was there a need for this to be written? (Identify the purpose)

- What is the conclusion?

You don't have to get theological about these questions. Considering these questions will help to bring understanding and revelation. Using a concordance or Bible dictionary helps to better understand the actual meaning of a scripture passage. A Bible concordance can help you better understand something more specific. For instance, perhaps you desire more revelation on finances. You can use a Bible concordance to look up scriptures regarding money and what the Lord says about wealth and prosperity.

God can and will show you something about you or your life in every scripture if you ask Him. As you pray for understanding about the Scripture verse, passage, or chapter that applies to your personal life situations, here are some questions to consider and put in your journal.

- What is the passage saying to me?
- Lord, what do you want to say to me today?
- What sin is revealed that I need to confess?
- How have I disobeyed God?
- What is the warning?
- What is God's command?
- What is God's promise?
- What is the condition for receiving the promise?
- What are the specific instructions?
- What should I thank and praise God for?

Memorization

One way to use Scripture in everyday life is to memorize key passages. Key passages include God's promises, His commands, and warnings, scriptures that bring peace and express God's love. Special scripture God illuminates during your time together. Why do you want to memorize scripture? So you are ready for whatever life throws at you.

A doctor told me I had thyroid cancer and needed surgery to cut out a lump in my throat. He said I would have to eat and speak from a tube in my throat for the rest of my life. I memorized 1 Peter 2:24 which says, *"who Himself bore our sins in His own body on the tree, that we, having died to sins, might live for righteousness—by whose stripes you were healed."* I didn't have the surgery, and they decided they were wrong about thyroid cancer. There are no tubes in my throat. A few months later, doctors told me I had breast cancer. I already had the verse memorized and began once again to speak that verse and meditate on it. The doctors returned a diagnosis saying they had made an error and there was no cancer. A year later I was told I had a brain tumor. Guess what scripture I immediately declared? 1 Peter 2:24. I have MRI pictures of a brain tumor, but in my brain, there is no longer a brain tumor. Scripture works, and to win the battles life throws your way, you need the Word of God hiding and ready in your heart. If you need help with memorizing scripture, here are a few tips and ideas that will help.

- There are some great apps that help with Bible verse memorizations. I use an app called Bible Memory.

- If you don't like apps, try this: Write the verse and reference on an index card.

- Seek understanding. Read the verse in its context. For instance, for John 15:5 you might read John 15:1-17. Meditate on the verse and ask God in prayer to help you understand what it means.

- Read the verse aloud several times. Practice speaking it to yourself.

- Learn to quote the verse one phrase at a time. Divide the verse into short and meaningful phrases. Learn to quote the first phrase Word for Word. Then build on it by learning the second phrase. Continue until you can quote the entire verse, Word for Word.

- Repeat the verse to another person. They probably need to hear it too!

- Review the memorized verse regularly. During the first week, carry the card with you. Pull it out for review several times daily during waiting periods, like riding in an elevator, riding to work, getting your coffee, or lunch break.

- Review the verse as often as you need to.

- Put the verse to music or find a song written about the verse. Sometimes it's easier to remember a verse when it's in a song. You can probably still remember songs you knew years ago. Music is a powerful tool to help you memorize, and it's very much okay if you make up songs to help you remember.

- We have talked several times about keeping a journal and the importance of taking notes. Our minds are amazing but sometimes forgetful. When you keep a record of the things God shows you as you meditate on the Word, you will be able to go back to it and rehearse your revelations and inspirations, helping you through tough times. Here are some things to consider writing as the scriptures help you through various times.

    - What did you learn?

    - What do you want to remember?

    - What does the scripture mean?

    - How does it apply to you?

One important element of meditating on God's Word is what to do with it once you've read it. The answer is simple. Obedience. Obeying the things you have learned nurtures spiritual growth and glorifies God. Being obedient to the Word means that you are following and doing the things you learn.

Summing It Up

We can sum up reading and meditating on the Word of God in a few brief steps.

- Quiet yourself, becoming still before the Lord eliminating distractions.

- Tune into the Holy Spirit allowing the Spirit to flow through your imagination and heart thus using your spiritual eyes and ears to bring you a revelation of the scripture.

- Feel God's heart for you asking the Lord what the Scripture reveals about His heart toward you and listening to His response.

- Write it down. Take the time to journal your conversation with the Lord, recording what He shows you and tells you about the Scripture. This is His Rhema (spoken) word that is just for you.

- Act on His Rhema word to you. This is one reason you need to write it down. You need to remember what the Lord said to you so you can do what He asks you to do.

- Remember, the Word of God is a love letter to you. He wants to show you how much He loves you and all that He does for you.

He wants to help you through good and bad times. Most of all, He wants to show you how to live forever with Him. Each time you open the Scriptures, look for God's love. He wants to show you.

- Rejoice! You were not left alone. He is always with you and as you hide more and more scripture in your heart, you will see Him in every situation and become accustomed to being the living Word of God yourself.

"You are our epistle written in our hearts, known and read by all men; clearly you are an epistle of Christ, ministered by us, written not with ink but by the Spirit of the living God, not on tablets of stone but on tablets of flesh, that is, of the heart," 2 Corinthians 3:2-3.

Helpful Tools

The following are some tools that are available that make Bible study easier. They are resources that can be found in bookstores and online. These are by no means exclusive. There are many, many resources to help you. Look around and find what works best for you. There are many versions of the Bible as well. There are so many versions there will be a version that fits the way you interact with the Lord.

- Reference Study Bible: <u>Thompson Chain Reference</u>

- Bible Dictionary: Unger's Bible Dictionary or Zondervan

- Bible Commentary: <u>Jamison, Faucet and Brown Bible Commentary</u>

- Topical Bible: <u>Nave's Topical Bible</u>

- <u>Manners and Customs of the Bible</u> by J. I. Packer and Merrill C. Tenney

- Bible Concordance: <u>Strong's Exhaustive Concordance</u>

- <u>Scripture Keys for Kingdom Living</u> by June Newman Davis

Internet Resources

http://www.biblegateway.com/

http://www.blueletterbible.org/

http://www.eliyah.com/lexicon.html

http://www.biblehub.com/

http://bibleresources.bible.com/passagesearch.php

https://www.bible.com/

Stepping Stones

1. God gives all Scripture for you and makes them personal.

2. There are sixty-six books in the Bible, all an expression of God's love.

3. Religion kills.

4. God instructs you to rely on the Holy Spirit to illumine scripture for your benefit.

5. Approach the Word humbly and in faith.

6. Meditate on scripture day and night.

7. Keep your heart holy and pure before God.

8. Keep scripture in context.

9. Remember, the scriptures are personal. Ask God what He is saying to you.

10. Be a living epistle read of all men.

Love Letters from God

Walking in the Word

1. Give two scriptures that explain why you should spend time in the Bible.

2. How many books in the Bible? _____

    a. How many Old Testament books? _____

    b. How many New Testament books? _____

3. What benefits are there from meditating on the Bible?

4. What are two tips that would help with your Bible study time?

5. Consider your own Bible study time. What steps can you take to improve this time with the Lord?

Glossary

SIMPLE GLOSSARY OF A FEW WORDS FROM THE CHRISTIAN FAITH

Adultery - The act of being sexually unfaithful to one's spouse

Agape - Affection, goodwill, love, brotherly love, a love feast

Angel - Messenger of God

Apostasy - Turning away from the religion, faith, or principles that one used to believe

Apostle - One sent forth, one chosen and sent with a special commission as a fully authorized representative of the sender.

Atonement - To cover, blot out, forgive; restore harmony between two individuals.

Attribute – An inherent characteristic

Backslide - To go back to ungodly ways of believing or acting.

Blasphemy - Words or actions showing a lack of respect for God or anything sacred.

Bless - To make or call holy; to ask God's favor, to praise; to make happy.

Blessing - A prayer asking God's favor for something, something that brings joy or comfort.

Born-again – To be begotten or birthed from God, the beginning, to start anew

Carnal - Of the flesh or body, not of the spirit, worldly; seat of one's desires opposed to the spirit of Christ

Cherubim - Guardian angels, angels that guard or protect places

Commitment - A promise, a pledge

Conditional - Placing restrictions, conditions, or provisions to receive

Conversion - Turn, return, turn back; change

Convert - To change from one form or use to another, to change from one belief or religion to another.

Courtship - The act or process of seeking the affection of one with the intent of seeking to win a pledge of marriage

Covenant - A pledge, alliance, agreement

Cult - A body of believers whose doctrine denies the deity of Christ.

Deliverance - A freeing or being freed, rescue; the act of change or transformation.

Demon - Evil spirit

Devil - Principal title for satan, the archenemy of God and man

Dispensation - A period of time, sometimes called ages

Dominion - To rule over, have power over, overcome, exercise lordship over

Eros - Erotic, physical love

Eternal - Existing always, forever, without time

Evangelist - Proclaims the gospel of Jesus Christ

Faith - Believing, trusting, depending, and relying on God

Fellowship - Sharing, communion, partnership, intimacy

Forgiveness - To pardon, release from bondage

Fornication - To act like a harlot, to be unfaithful to God, illicit sexual intercourse

Glorification - Salvation of the body, transforming mortal bodies to eternal bodies

Grace - Unmerited favor of God, help given in the time of need from a loving God

Holy - Set apart, sacred

Intercession - To meet or encounter, to strike upon, to pray for another

Justification - Salvation of the spirit, just as if I never sinned

Marriage - A divine institution designed by God as an intimate union, which is physical, emotional, intellectual, social, and most importantly, spiritual

New Testament - Text of the new covenant

Offering - Everything you give beyond your tithe

Old Testament - Text of the old covenant

Omnipotent - All-encompassing power of God

Omnipresent - Unlimited nature of God, ability to be everywhere at all times

Omniscient - God's power to know all things

Pastor - Shepherds of the body of believers

Philia - Conditional love, based on feelings, friendships

Praise - Thanksgiving, to say good things about, words that show approval.

Prayer - Communication with God

Prophet - One who is a spokesperson for God, one who has seen the message of God and declares that message

Propitiation - To satisfy the anger of God, to gain favor; appease

Rapture - To be carried away, or the catching away of

Reconciliation - Restore harmony or fellowship between individuals, to make friendly again

Redemption - To buy back, to purchase, recover, to Rescue from sin

Regeneration - To give new life or force to, renew, to be restored, to make better, improve or reform, to grow back anew

Repent - To give new life or force, to renew, to be restored, to make better, improve or reform, to grow back a new.

Resurrection - A return to life subsequent to death

Revelation - The act of revealing or making known

Righteousness - Right standing with God, integrity, virtue, purity of life, correctness of thinking

Sacrifice - The act of offering something, giving one thing for the sake of another; a loss of profit

Salvation - Deliverance from any kind of evil whether material or spiritual, being saved from danger or evil; to rescue.

Sanctification - Salvation of the soul. Separation from the seduction of sin

Satan - The chief of fallen spirits, opponent; adversary

Sealing - Something that guarantees, a sign or token, to make with a seal to make it official or genuine

Sin - All unrighteousness, missing the mark, wrong or fault; violation of the law

Spirit - A being that is not of this world, has no flesh or bones

Steward - A guardian or overseer of someone else's property, manager

Supernatural - Departing from what is usual, normal, or natural to give the appearance of transcending the laws of nature

Talent - A natural skill that is unusual.

Tithe - Ten percent of all your increase

Tribulation - Distress, trouble, a pressing together, pressure, affliction

Trinity - Three in one: Father, Son, Holy Spirit

Unconditional - No restrictions, conditions, boundaries, demands, or specific provisions

Will – Choice, inclination, desire, pleasure, command, what one wishes or determines shall be done

About the Author

Pamela is a teacher, mentor, and author of the inspirational book *Destiny Arise* and children's books including *Time in a Tuna*. Pam earned her bachelor's degree at the University of Illinois Springfield, her master's degree in Organizational Leadership at Lincoln Christian University, and her doctorate in Leadership at Christian Leadership University. She serves as a mentor for the Spirit Life Circles sponsored by CLU.

She works from her home in the prairie land of central Illinois. Pam and her bodybuilding husband own a gym/fitness center that promotes living a balanced life. She taught sixth grade for almost twenty years. Pam also taught preschool through adult-age students in various venues. She served as director of Super Church, the children's ministry in the United Methodist Church in her hometown. Pam also served in the church nursery, as director of New Life Ministries Discipleship Program, Vacation Bible School Director, Kingdom Kids Children's Ministry Director, and Sunday School teacher. She has also been on missionary trips. Her favorite trip, so far, was the time she spent in Belize.

Pam enjoys kayaking, bicycling, and riding her motor scooter. When she isn't writing, she enjoys spending time with her four children and their families which includes five grandchildren who are the inspiration of her children's books.

Walking with Jesus Series

Becoming the Best Me I Can Be

Book 1 - There Must Be a Better Way
Walking in Salvation

Book 2 - Lord, I Need Help!
Walking with the Holy Spirit

Book 3 - I Thought I Was Changed
Walking in Transformation

Book 4 - I Am Supernatural
Walking in Spiritual Gifts

Book 5 - I Am Strong
Walking as a Warrior

Book 6 - I Am Fruitful
Walking in the Fruit of the Spirit

Book 7 - Love Letters from God
Walking in the Word

Book 8 - Time in the Garden
Walking in the Power of Prayer

Book 9 - I'm in Charge of What?
Walking in Stewardship

Book 10 - The End of – Well, Pretty Much Everything
Walking into Eternity

Who am I? What am I doing here? Where am I going? Everyone at some point in life asks these questions. You were wired to ask and engineered to pursue the answers. The road to discovering destiny is besieged by fiascoes, failures, and the agony of defeat. If your strength has been depleted and has caused you to give up, sit down, push pause, and snooze until another day, then this book is just for you! Amazing experiences are waiting for you. Get ready to be awakened from the posture of defeat, depression, and despair.

Destiny Arise is an easy-to-read book, providing tools to aid in living an amazing life. This book is designed as a trip adviser for your expedition. It will teach you how to evict the spirit of mediocrity and use your past to propel you into your future. You will learn how to shake off the common, arising to be an uncommon force taking your rightful place in the earth. You can change the world. I pray this book will ignite a passionate fire to pursue your destiny unapologetically. Destiny, awake from your slumber and arise.

www.ingramcontent.com/pod-product-compliance
Lightning Source LLC
Chambersburg PA
CBHW062158100526
44589CB00014B/1872